"Maybe the best moment of your life will be on your next big adventure…"

If you would like to check out more recipes and campervan tips please pop on to **my website** www.thecampercookie.com

See Youtube, thecampercookie, for recipes and updates on our campervan conversion

You could also check out my **Instagram** pictures to see more pictures of our adventures at *thecampercookie*

ISBN 978-1-9999009-0-8

Adventures of a Lazy Campervan Cook

Summer Bourne

'The Camper Cookie'

Other Books by Summer Bourne:

Simple but delicious recipes especially for campervan meals (or for cooking at home on a busy week day!)

Contents

Campervan Tip No 1: Screw a little mug hook in to the edge of the surface that you prepare food at. You can then hang a plastic carrier bag by one handle from the hook for easy disposal of the veg peelings and any bits of rubbish as you cook.

Living the Dream…

When people talk about *living the dream* they often use it describe owning a campervan, and you'll get no argument from me on that. I just LOVE the thrill of setting off in a campervan, even if it is only for a weekend, because what we are doing when we do this is… *starting an adventure.*

But why is it so exciting? Living in a small campervan for a few days or, for some people, a few years is not really a comfortable experience, let's face it. You are often sleeping in a smaller than normal bed, you may have headroom but you may not, you often have to shower in washrooms (if you get a shower at all), toilet-life can be challenging and sometimes the weather is just grim and you get cold and wet. It certainly isn't like spending your holiday in a luxury hotel but nobody seems to speak longingly about spending a night in a hotel in the way they do about a campervan trip. A hotel, no matter how gorgeous, is not an adventure.

Over the four years that we have been camping in our micro-campervan, 'Trev-the-Prev', Glyn and I have had some amazing adventures and seen and done things we would normally never have done. Our life, as campervanners, has been completely different to our life as non-campervanners. We now look forward to the summer in a way we didn't before and, every year brings new possibilities and places to see. Life is just richer with a campervan.

There is also something delicious and dead cosy about having your own little home on wheels and it is hard not to become fond of your van which is probably why everybody gives their van a name. You can decorate it how you want it and you get to know every little inch of it as you share your adventures together.

The FREEDOM

But, I think that what people are mostly talking about when they describe *living the dream* in a van is the *FREEDOM.* I guess, deep down inside, we are all still hunter-gatherers and a part of our genetic code still longs to roam. Many of us sit in offices every week with predictable routines and have days that hold no surprises. No matter how much we might love our job, there are few better feelings than, on a Friday night, knowing you've finished work for 48 hours and the next two days are your own. With a van, you can just take off and go wherever you want and forget about that day-to-day life for a while.

You also get to re-experience what if feels like to be spontaneous again which is nectar for the soul. For me, there is nothing more exciting than stepping out of the van in the morning knowing that you can do anything you like, go anywhere you like and change your direction at any point along the way.

The other deep joy about campervan life is getting outside and back in to Nature again. And, with a camper, you get to immerse yourself in the wild outdoors but still enjoy the comforts of home, even if it is in a cut-down form. You have your cosy little bed to sleep in, your cute little stove to cook on, and, if you are like us, you even have a TV so you can do a box-set binge. What's not to like!

We have had many funny, soulful and just plain gorgeous moments in our campervan over the past few years, exploring this beautiful little island of ours and, in the years to come, we hope to explore other countries as well. So many adventures, so little time! Sometimes I really envy those people who are retired who can just take off and come home to their own rhythm. But good luck to them, I say.

Most Surprising Adventure

However, one of the biggest and most surprising adventures for me in this time is that I have become a campervan cook who writes a blog and books on the subject, something that I would never have seen myself doing in a million years. In fact, I have now become a bit of a campervan geek and we are converting our next campervan ourselves as we now know exactly what we want in a van (within a certain budget or course, sigh!) and exactly what we *don't* want.

So, come with me and I'll share with you some of the adventures that we have had in Trev-the-Prev so far and some of the 'lazy' recipes that I have found along the way that are definitely made for adventures in a campervan.

Happy Vanning!

Summer

How it All Started…

"Oh no, I don't believe it!"

We had just pulled in to the Taunton services on the M5 on our way down to Cornwall and, as I wandered around the shop trying not to buy a load of tat that I didn't need or would ever need, I noticed the front-page headlines in the Daily Express:

'2 MONTHS RAIN IN A WEEK'

As I carried on reading, it got worse:

5

'Britain faces a week of torrential rain and 80mph gales as a series of storms roll in from the Atlantic. Up to 5ins of rain – almost two months' worth – could lead to flooding, particularly in the South.'

This was 2013 and our first ever trip in a campervan, or to be more precise, a motorhome and we were heading off for a week's camping in the West Country.

Glyn, my partner, and I had been camping for many years in our tent, but we were getting a bit fed up with putting the tent up in the half light on a Friday evening (including the inevitable tired-and-tetchy argument) and taking down a wet tent in the rain when we left. But I do LOVE camping.

Why we had never thought about getting a campervan before I do not know but I guess it is for the same reason that many people don't think about it even though they would secretly love to – they assume that they just can't afford it. And when it comes to the glossy, sexy Vdubs that you see at the shows this is probably true but, there is a way that you can 'live the *(campervan)* dream' on a very tight budget and I'll tell you more about that later.

For now, we had a motorhome for a week courtesy of Groupon. It was one of the big, white coachbuilts (don't ask me which model it was as I wasn't a campervan geek at that time and never even noticed) and, as it was on a Groupon, it wasn't one of their best rentals anyway, but it was exciting for us. As we drove down the motorway it rattled alarmingly like bits were about to drop off at any minute but it all stayed intact, so I guess that that is just how the older models behave.

Our Mysterious Theme for the Week

We decided to have a theme to our week away and planned to visit some of the sites mentioned in a book I had read (see below) that talked about an energy alignment which weaves across Britain from St Michaels Mount in Cornwall all the way up to Hopton on the Norfolk coast. This line passes through some really interesting historical locations, especially sacred sites and churches, often dedicated to St Michael or St Mary, and I thought that this would take us to some unusual and beautiful places. We had our bikes strapped on the back so planned to go off exploring too. Anyway, that was the plan. But now they were promising gales and extreme weather, so this was going to be interesting.

We carried on down to Cornwall and found a nice site near St Michael's Mount but I don't remember much about that first morning other than I felt more wrecked when I got up than when I went to bed. First off, the beds. This was one of the classic motorhomes with the double bed above the cabin and it felt a bit like sleeping in an MRI scanner. I'm not claustrophobic but this wasn't for me. Also, I am one of those people who usually needs a pee in the night and this would have meant navigating a sheer drop on a ladder that was clearly made for a hamster cage. For the rest of the trip I slept in one of the bunk beds at the back which was okay as I am little enough to fit in to child-sized beds, but it wasn't the most romantic of holidays. Added to this, the promised rain and the gales had finally hit our area which made the van shake and rattle all night and I suddenly knew what it must be like to sleep in a tumble-drier. So, the next morning we were not at our best. However, I was CAMPING and I was not going to let these things spoil our adventures.

Going Wild and Wilder

The next night we decided to go wild and we spent the night in the car park of a lovely little church in a pretty out-of-the-way village. I always think that small church car parks are a good bet for an overnight stop so long as you are not there on Sunday morning of course. However, fate struck again and we were woken up at 7am

7

to what sounded like Armageddon. Workmen with diggers and jack-hammers had arrived to do work on the road opposite so there was no lie-in that day. However, it was a good excuse to get the bikes out and go for a lovely ride around the moor and then come back and find a little café for lunch.

For the rest of the week the gales continued but it didn't stop us visiting some great places like Bodmin moor, St Michael's Mount, Penzance, Lostwithiel (amazing ancient church here) and The Saints Way, an old pilgrimage route.

We finished the week at a very special place on the Cornwall-Devon border called Brentor. There is a very unusual church here that clings to the top of a craggy outcrop apparently made from solidified lava from a volcano that was active there when it was under the sea (yes, Devon – really!). From a distance, it seems very dark and brooding, like something out of *The Woman in Black*, and it is very atmospheric. The church is quite simple and is dedicated to St. Michael and has an amazing stained-glass window depicting the arch-angel Michael. The church is actually called St. Michel du Rupe which means Michael of the Rock.

We Were Now Addicted

As we sat in the church on our last day I felt quite thrilled by our experience of being in a motorhome and knew that I was totally addicted now. We needed to get own campervan, something much smaller, we realised, as we had found the motorhome quite restrictive down the little West Country roads and we were getting a bit fed-up of being glared at in supermarket car parks, but get something we must. We didn't know how we were going to manage it then as we just didn't have the funds for even an older campervan but, I guess St Michael must have been listening as a 'campervan' did come along and find us and it was something I couldn't have even imagined at that time. It's funny how life can be quite magical sometimes…

Note: The Book I read is: 'The Sun and the Serpent' by Paul Broadhurst & Hamish Miller

THE RECIPE:

One-Pot Pasta Genovese

I wasn't a campervan cook at that time, but it was on this trip that I put together my first campervan recipe. It is a very simple one and is a good standby even today.

SMALL, NEW POTATOES (SKIN ON) CHOPPED INTO QUARTERS (HALF A KILO WHICH IS ROUGHLY HALF A BAG)

FINE GREEN BEANS CHOPPED INTO 1" PIECES (150G WHICH IS ABOUT HALF A BAG)

DRIED PASTA SUCH AS FUSILLI OR PENNE (200G WHICH IS ABOUT A THIRD OF A BAG)

1 POT OF FRESH GREEN PESTO (150G) OR AROUND 3 TABLESPOONS OF PESTO FROM A JAR

How to cook:

Heat around 1.5 litres of water in a large saucepan until boiling and add the chopped potatoes to the water. Cook for 10 minutes.

Add the chopped green beans and the pasta to the water and let it cook for another 10 minutes. Drain the water off.

Add the pesto to the saucepan and mix with the potatoes, beans and pasta until all are well coated and serve

This dish is great served with crusty bread or a green salad and is nice cold the next day.

Campervan Tip No 2: If you are travelling to your campsite or wild spot and you know that you are going to arrive late, have the van ready in 'sleep mode' before you leave. This means having the bed made up, any blinds ready and easy to find, hot drink equipment easy to get to and pack the bigger equipment (such as awning, chairs) in the order that you need to take them out at the other end.

Say Hello to 'Trev-the-Prev'...

Like an over-excited child, I began to search online for campervans for sale and Glyn and I also went to a few motorhome/campervan shows to see what was on offer. My heart sank. The vans we saw at the shows were way out of our financial league and any van that I had found online that we could afford looked as though it would probably do a couple of hundred miles and keel over.

We had very little spare cash at the time as Glyn was still paying maintenance for his children which took a large chunk out of our income. We weren't starving but it didn't leave much in the pot for a campervan fund. And then something magical happened. To this day I have no memory of how I came across the information but, somehow, I became aware of Bumble Campers – a small campervan rental and conversion company in Peterborough. I guess I must have come across them online somehow and I was amazed to see that they offered campervans (well, camper-cars) for under £3000. James Kelly has been running Bumble for many years mainly as a campervan rental business for Toyota Previas, a bit like *Wicked* do in Australia – you know, the company with all the bright, graffiti Previa campervans. (Interesting Fact: I was told that, at one point, *Wicked* had a Previa camper on their books with over 500,000 miles on the clock that was still going strong! I don't know how true that is but Previas are known for just going and going. As they say, "You can't kill a Previa").

Like many people do when they first see a Previa campervan, I thought that there just couldn't be enough room in there for a real bed or anything else but I was wrong. The bed we have in our Previa is one of the most comfortable beds I have ever slept in and I always get a great night's sleep in the van. I know the standard rock and roll beds look the bees' knees but I don't find them comfortable, neither wide enough or soft enough. My friends who had a deluxe Nissan camper conversion with a rock and roll bed could only sleep on it with a considerable depth of memory foam. I have seen the top-end rock and roll beds that are available now (I believe they cost around £2000) and I must admit they do look comfortable, but you need a wider space and a wider budget.

We had a chat to James and he suggested the best way to find out if a Previa conversion was for us was to try one out as a rental for a weekend and he offered us a good rate for this. I'm a great believer in trying a van before you make that final commitment although, having said that, at the time of writing this book we are converting our new panel van (Vauxhall Vivaro) and I have no idea if we are going to like it as a camper when it's done as there is no way of trying it out first. But I guess that is part of the adventure.

Trying out the New Van

Glyn and I set off for Peterborough and collected our rental home-on-wheels for the weekend. We didn't do anything too extreme for those couple of days, just mooched around the general area and went on nice walks as it was more about the van than the holiday. And we loved it.

"Life is simple. Eat. Sleep. Camp."

James had given us one of his more up-spec vans which had an electric sunroof in the back and it was lovely to lie in bed and look at the stars at night. I was also surprised how easy it was to drive as I wasn't used to driving automatics but, once I got used to the length of it, it was a very relaxed drive. We decided that we really wanted the higher spec Previa (the GLX) with the sunroof and cruise control but James said that they were not so easy to find. What followed was a couple of months of us all looking out for a decent GLX model for James to convert.

Eventually, Glyn and I found one at a Toyota dealer in London who specialised in fancy Toyota imports and had an older Previa on his forecourt from a part exchange that he wanted to get rid of. We paid the man £900 and 'Trev-The-Prev' came in to our lives.

We left Trev with James at Bumble for a few weeks and then went to collect him in his new incarnation in the spring of 2014 to get ready for our first year's campervanning. Our new campervan had cost us £2,500 in total.

At this time, I still had no idea that I would end up as a campervan-foodie blogger and cookbook writer as my mind was just racing with ideas for planning some trips away. You just never know what is just around the corner.

THE RECIPE:

Chilli con Beanie

Many years ago, I spent a few years as a vegetarian, not because of any great ethical reasons (although I don't like to see animals suffer) but because my body simply went off meat. It was almost as much a surprise to me as anyone else. This meant that I had to learn a lot of new recipes and adapt some of the ones I already cooked into non-meat versions. One of the most successful adaptations was my Chilli con Beanie, a no-meat version of Chilli con Carne. It is so easy and tasty that I have cooked it ever since even though I am an omnivore again. Because it is a one-pot dish it is great as a campervan meal and it is one I often make before we go off in the van so that we can take it with us and just heat it up when we arrive at our campsite, usually late in the evening. We normally just want to get set up and relax and can't be bothered to cook or go and find a pub. It is one of those meals that almost tastes better the next day and any leftovers make a great filling for quesadilla.

OIL FOR FRYING (2 TBSPS)

1 LARGE GREEN PEPPER (CHOPPED IN TO SMALL PIECES)

1 MEDIUM ONION (CHOPPED IN TO SMALL PIECES)

1 CAN OF PLUM TOMATOES (400G)

1 PACKET OF CHILLI CON CARNE SPICE MIX

1 CAN KIDNEY BEANS (400G)

1 CAN MIXED BEANS (400G) OR ANY OTHER BEANS THAT YOU LIKE: e.g HARICOT

How to Make

Heat the oil in a large saucepan and add the chopped pepper. Fry for 2~3 minutes. Add the chopped onion and fry until both are soft.

Add the tin of plum tomatoes. Cook a little and break them up until the mixture is smooth.

Add the Chilli spice mix, stir and add some water if it is too thick. Let this mixture cook gently for 5 minutes.

Add the drained can of kidney beans and the drained can of mixed beans. Let this cook gently for around 10 minutes, stirring occasionally so that it doesn't stick to the bottom.

Serve with a dollop of natural yogurt and a sprinkling of grated mature cheddar. You can eat it by itself or with rice and it's also nice on toast or on a baked potato (if you are cooking it at home). It also tastes good the following day and freezes well.

Campervan Tip No 3: Have an easy-reach place where you always put you van keys at night so you know exactly where they are in an emergency. It also means that you don't have to do the annoying hunt-the-keys game when you are setting off in the morning

How to Make 'Special' Friends Without Trying…

Do You Come Here Often?

Our first ever trip out in Trev was to Cardiff in Wales. We thought that we wouldn't go too far for our first trip while we got used to the van (we live in Wiltshire) so we decided to have a quirky weekend on an evening ghost walk in Llandaff which is a rather special 'village' on the outskirts of Cardiff. If you haven't been to Llandaff it is definitely worth a visit. It has a long history going back to the 6th century and has an amazing cathedral there which is worth a look at but Llandaff has now become a suburb of the city although it still retains its village feel. With so much history it's no surprise that the area has a fair amount of ghost stories. A "Road of the dead" ran behind the cathedral, where bodies were carried along the river. Tales also include ghostly soldiers, monks and priests, a white lady, the faceless man in black, an ugly witch-demon, and curious spirit children. So, we were really intrigued to see what might happen on our ghost walk which started at the cathedral green just after dark.

We had decided to 'go wild' for camping that night so we arrived in the afternoon to find the village and check it out and then go and find a spot for the night as the tour didn't finish until around 11pm and we didn't want to be driving around in the dark trying to find somewhere to park up then.

We found a lovely little spot, a small, country park car park, on the outskirts of the city. It was a really pretty place on the edge of a wood where people were walking their dogs and there was even a sculpture trail which we thought we would explore the next morning after breakfast.

With that sorted we went back to Llandaff and had an amazing meal at a tucked-away restaurant (no longer there unfortunately) and then gathered on the village green for our walk. It was a really interesting tour as our guide was a good storyteller (and was writing a thesis on psychopaths which was fascinating to learn about, too) and the place was very atmospheric at night. We didn't encounter any ghosts although there was a strange moment when we were walking along by the cathedral. The air became very cold and we could all see our breath mist-up as we exhaled even though it was a warm night.

It was a good evening but Glyn and I were tired now and ready to get in to our campervan bed for the first time so we drove back to our little car park for the night. We parked up and put the kettle on for a cup of tea. As we sat there we heard a car pull up and park on the other side of the car park which we thought was a bit odd for nearly midnight. The driver turned off the engine and just sat there. We weren't too comfortable with this and were wondering if this might be a drug dealing spot or something (I grew up in London and drug dealing is often done in the parks there).

Then another car pulled up and went and parked near the first one. It was clear the drivers were familiar with this as they seemed to know exactly what to do. Then another car came and parked up and left it's lights on. Suddenly it dawned on us – this was a 'dogging' spot (I will let Mr Google explain that if it is necessary!). I think we were about to make a whole bunch of new friends who would probably see Trev as a very comfortable place to 'get to know each other'.

It was now gone midnight and Glyn and I realised we were going to have to find another place for the night but had no idea where to go so just headed back to Llandaff and parked up on the green there. One of the advantages of having a converted Toyota Previa is that nobody thinks it could possibly be a campervan so stealth camping is no problem.

By now Glyn and I were both *very* tired and we wearily started converting Trev into night mode which wasn't that easy considering this was the first time that we had done it. The blinds in Trev are ones that stick on to the windows with plastic suckers and, being an MPV, there were a lot of windows to stick blinds on to and they were all different shapes and sizes. It was a bit like a Tetris puzzle and I think it was gone 1am by the time we got to bed, a bit dazed with the weirdness of it all.

Having avoided 'new friends' at the car park were we now going to make 'new friends' of the ethereal kind while we slept near the haunted cathedral? Luckily that didn't happen and we actually got a good night's sleep and it was quite good fun to wake up in the morning and have a cup of tea on the green.

I will always remember Llandaff fondly as it is a fascinating place but I'm glad that we didn't come back with any special friends, of the human *or* ghostly kind.

The Mystery of 'Room No 2'

And then, three years on, there was another mysterious incident where we seemed to have unintentionally made 'friends' of the intimate kind again.

In September 2017, we spent a weekend in Abergavenny in Wales (maybe it's a Welsh thing?) to visit The Abergavenny Food Festival. It's a bit like the Edinburgh fringe festival except that, instead of the town being covered in comedy, it is given over to fantastic food of every kind. There are food stalls all through the streets selling cooked meals and local produce and lots of talks and workshops on everything food. I was in heaven! I even managed to do a food photography course that showed how you can get amazing shots from your smartphone. I often struggle to 'stage' my food at home when I am doing a photograph of a recipe as I eat everything I cook and, frankly, I'm hungry and I can't wait (there has also been many a time when I have had to wrestle Glyn's dinner off him to photograph it first). So, anything that means I can take a picture quicker and easier is fine by me.

Anyway, we camped at a pretty, farm campsite a few miles away (you know, the type that almost feels like you are wild camping) and drove in to the festival each day. They had set up a special festival car park in some fields on the edge of town so it was possible to park there and just walk in.

We had a great day at the festival and I discovered a supplier for fabulous apple cider vinegar with 'mother' (see recipe below), some wasabi plants which I am going to grow for salad leaves, a new mission to discover an easy way to cook Welsh cakes in the van and some of the best olive oil I have ever tasted. I won't bore you with all the things that we ate and drank throughout the day as well but, yes, it was a lot. All in all, it was a great day.

"I don't need therapy, I just need to go camping."

As we walked back to Trev with all our goodies we suddenly became aware that something wasn't right. As we approached the van Glyn noticed that there was an 'open door' light on the dashboard and, as we are very careful about locking up the van when we leave it, we knew that somebody must have been in the van while we weren't there. My heart sank. Not only is it horrible to think of somebody going inside your van, like the invasion you feel when somebody burgles your house, but our special 12v/240v TV and my new laptop were in the van along with all our personal items of course.

We realised that the open door was the hatch at the back which is where our kitchen unit is. We opened the hatch but everything looked exactly as we had left it. I looked throughout the van and nothing had been stolen or broken. And then we noticed a key on the shelf at the back of the van. It was a rounded key with a white fob on it that simply said, 'Room No 2'. It was clearly the key to a hotel or B&B room which somebody had quietly left in the back of our van?!?

Now I know what you are probably thinking and we were thinking the same thing too. In fact, when we handed the key to one of the festival stewards the next day he did laugh and asked us if we had made any 'special friends' while we were at the festival to which we replied, "Definitely Not" (I think we may be getting a bit of a reputation in Wales!). So, to the person in '*Room No 2*', I'm sorry if you were expecting a visitor or visitors that night and you feel like you were stood-up but I'm afraid you left the key in the wrong car!

THE RECIPE:

Super-food Beetroot Salad

1 MEDIUM RAW BEETROOT

1 MEDIUM SWEET APPLE

JUICE OF 1 LEMON

1 TSP OF APPLE CIDER VINEGAR WITH MOTHER*

How to Make

You just grate the beetroot and apple in to a bowl, cover with the lemon juice and mix in the apple cider vinegar. And that's it! I like a lot of lemon juice but you may want to adjust that according to how big and juicy your lemon is. You can also leave out the apple cider vinegar if you don't have it to hand but it is so good for you and tastes great.

You can have this micro-salad on the side with any main salad you are making and it goes really well with burgers for some reason. Just experiment and, like I say, sometimes you can just eat it on its own or have it as a pre-salad to a meal.

*Apple cider vinegar (ACV) with the mother is simply unrefined, unpasteurized and unfiltered ACV. The "mother" is a colony of beneficial bacteria which helps keep our digestion working properly.

So Why am I a 'Lazy' Cook...

Lazy is an interesting word.

The first thing most people think about when they are told that someone is lazy is that they are a person who is not willing to work or do any activity that needs effort. They are not really pulling their weight and we feel, maybe, a bit of contempt for their laziness.

But 'lazy' has another side to it. Think about the idea of 'a lazy summer's day' or a 'lazy Sunday' and you get a whole different flavour. In this case lazy is quite delicious and talks about something that is slow and relaxed with a hint of a languid smile (I love the word languid as it makes me think of molten, shiny chocolate and anything that has rivers of chocolate flowing through it can't be bad).

In Denmark they have a special word that I think describes how I like to cook and eat food – it is *Hygge* (pronounced Hoo-ga). The Danes, who have been named as the happiest nation in the world, say there isn't really a direct translation into English as we just don't have one word that encompasses everything that Hygge is but the closest we come to it is *cosy*. Hygge also includes feeling safe, warm, togetherness and a general sense of wellbeing. This is an example of Hygge – you and your partner are staying in on a wild and wet evening. You have a log fire roaring in the fireplace and candles light the room. You are wearing your comfy pyjamas and you both curl up on the sofa with blankets, a cup of cocoa and a chocolate biscuit to watch a great film on TV. You get the picture.

So, when it comes to cooking, yes, I am a 'lazy' cook and try to bring the spirit of Hygge in to the whole thing. To me, cooking should be relaxed, easy and nourishing in a homely way. It should not be stressful, complicated or something that makes us feel bad about ourselves because we can't produce supermodel food like we see in many cookbooks or on TV. Like many of the supermodels that we see in magazines, the food in the cookbooks is re-touched, either on the set or later at the photographic stage. It's not uncommon for WD40 to be sprayed on the food to make it look shiny; come near my dinner with a can of WD40 and I will wrestle you to the ground, especially if it is one of my favourites like *'Avocado Crema'* (see below).

Of course, our food should try to look appetising as we eat with our eyes as well as our mouths and I do enjoy some of the beautiful food pictures that some recipe writers produce. For food photographs that almost look like paintings check out Jessie at *Life as A Strawberry*. But, like the pictures of supermodels, we need to remember that it isn't real life and I feel that we should get back to just producing nutritious, tasty meals in a relaxed and joyful way.

It's Hard to Cook Fancy in a Campervan

When you are out camping, it is a bit hard to be fancy anyway. A campervan/tent/caravan kitchen is limited in many ways.

- You have limited equipment
- You have limited space to prepare and cook

- You have limited storage
- You have limited fuel
- You have limited water for washing-up

However, being able to still cook reasonably nutritious food when we are out on the road is something that is important to me. For many years I had a chronic illness that meant I had very little energy to get through the day and it was mainly studying nutrition that eventually enabled me to get well again. If only we realised the power of food to make us sick or keep us healthy! As Hippocrates said, - *"Let food be thy medicine and let medicine be thy food."*

So, I started to adapt my recipes for a camping kitchen which meant that they had to be quick and easy. And, if this meant using some pre-prepared, healthy foods to do that I was not going to be snobbish about it. For example, one of my favourite done-for-you foods is chargrilled peppers in a jar, usually preserved in olive oil. The fact is, we are very unlikely to grill and peel peppers in a camping situation and, to be honest, I'm unlikely to do it at home too, especially when the jar products are so good. These peppers are great for so many recipes like pasta, quesadillas, sandwiches, wraps or just with some lovely mozzarella cheese and basil.

I learned another great life lesson from my illness and that was to spend my energy wisely. Having a very small energy bank account taught me to be selective about how and with whom I spend my energy generally. In a way, I had no choice but to become 'lazy' but now I do it consciously and you'd be surprised how much easier life becomes when you are selectively lazy. This doesn't mean that there are not times when I pour myself passionately in to whatever I am doing, but it does mean that I try not to get stuck on the fast-spinning hamster wheel. I believe we all need to be a little kinder to ourselves and learn how to comfortably step on and off that wheel.

Practise the Art of 'Lazy'

When we are out camping it is the perfect time to practise the art of 'lazy'. Don't you just love it when you have nowhere to rush off to and can just languish in bed, preferably with the van door open looking out at a gorgeous view. And then you get up and cook your bacon and eggs (why does bacon smell beyond good in the open air?) and sit around with a cup of tea and chat before you set off for your day's adventure.

And then there are the warm evenings spent next to the van eating your dinner outside with a glass of something in hand just sitting around chatting and putting the world to right. Although I have to admit that one of the camping joys for Glyn and I is to get cosy in the van once it gets dark, turn the TV on, and have a box-set binge or catch up on recent films.

I think campervan holidays should be a gorgeous mixture of full-on adventure and full-on lazy. And that means cooking quick and easy meals that still make us go "Yum". Of course, this is not just for when we are out in the van but also for when we are at home on a busy weekday.

So, I do encourage you to invite a bit more laziness in to your life too, not the unproductive kind but the kind that lets you relax, de-stress and enjoy the art of languid.

THE RECIPE:

Avocado Crema

Recipes don't get much lazier (or tastier) than this.

LARGE RIPE AVOCADO

JUICE OF 1 LIME

1 CLOVE OF GARLIC, MINCED

2 TBSPS OF NATURAL YOGHURT

1 TBSP OF RUNNY HONEY

A GOOD PINCH OF SALT

A HANDFUL OF FRESH CORIANDER ROUGHLY CHOPPED

How to Make

Scoop the flesh out of the avocado and put it in a bowl or large mug

Add the lime juice and mash with a fork

Add the garlic, yoghurt, honey, salt and coriander and stir until you have a smooth crema

You can serve this with so many things. It is great on toast in the morning especially with some Philadelphia cheese, smoked salmon or a poached egg. Use it as a side for burgers or any Tex Mex style food you are having. You can even dilute it with a little olive oil and use it as a salad dressing..

Campervan Tip No 4: When you are exploring a new location, it is a good idea to first find a coffee shop and have a cup of coffee (and a bit of cake, of course, you're on holiday!). While you are there you can ask your barista for local info and any good places to visit – they always seem to know.

A Completely Perfect Day…

Sometimes, just sometimes, Life decides to hand you a completely perfect day. This happened for me a few years ago when I was camping down on the Dorset coast for what turned out to be the most exquisite spring day I have ever seen.

My friend, Liz, lives in Devon and I live in Wiltshire so we don't get to meet up too often although we do try and arrange a day out together somewhere in the middle now and then. In recent years we have also met up for a couple of days down on the Dorset coast at the end of April to celebrate Liz's birthday. Liz is not really a camper so she gets a cheap, mid-week caravan deal and I take our campervan and spend a couple of days at my favourite campsite there, Highlands End (see details at bottom), where you can park your van right on the cliffs and have the most amazing sea views.

I had arrived the night before and had a lovely morning waking up to a beautiful sunny day and ate my breakfast sitting next to the van watching the ocean wake-up. I had even had one of my favourite, slightly quirky breakfasts: *'Marvo Cheese on Toast' (see below)*.

The plan was that Liz would drive to my campsite for late morning and we'd spend the day walking along the cliffs with a stop for lunch at one of our favourite restaurants, of course. I'm afraid that food and drink does feature a lot in our get togethers but what nicer way to catch up than over a great cup of coffee or a tasty lunch. Liz arrived and I made us a cafetiere of coffee as we decided to sit awhile by the van and chat and enjoy the view before setting off for lunch.

Walking Around 'Broadchurch'

We drove in to West Bay, a pretty harbour town, and parked up right next to the beach. Any of you who have watched the ITV drama, Broadchurch, will be really familiar with West Bay. This series, (which Glyn and I were addicted to) stars David Tennant and Olivia Colman who play police officers in a fictitious town called 'Broadchurch' and they solve various murder cases there. Most of the series is shot around West Bay and it feels a little strange walking around the town and seeing various places where certain scenes were shot. In fact, I could see the cliff hut where one of the 'murders' took place from my campervan pitch!

By now it was lunchtime so it was time to go and find somewhere to eat and chat again. Yes, there is a lot of chatting in this story as women friends who haven't seen each other for a while can easily talk for hours (days?) which is something that Glyn (an I expect many men) find strange and just incomprehensible.

One of our favourite restaurants on the Dorset coast is The Watch Tower in West Bay which is right on the beach and does fish to die for. It is a bit pricey but this day they were doing their 'Silver Surfer' special which is a £10 meal deal for those of us over a certain age. Neither Liz or I are silver and only just scraped in to the age bracket but we were going to make the most of it and had the most succulent plate of fish and chips I have ever tasted (I just can't work out what they do differently that makes their fish so gorgeous but it is). As it was Liz's birthday they also gave us a couple of glasses of prosecco for free which was a bit special too.

"Camping: when you spend a small fortune to live like a homeless person."

Now we were ready to take off over the cliffs for what turned out to be the most magical of walks. I don't know about you but I just love cliff walks above all others. There is something special about walking where the ocean meets the land and this day was extra special because the weather was like nothing I have experienced before or since. This was a softly warm day and there was an almost ethereal quality to the sky which was covered in a lavender haze and the sea was totally still. In fact, the whole world felt totally still, as if another dimension had temporarily slipped in to ours, and it did not feel like we were in Britain at all, more like somewhere in the Mediterranean.

We really lost our sense of time but eventually we realised that we had walked as far as we could manage and made our way back to the Bay. Tired but happy we drove back to the campsite and I made us one of my spontaneous risottos which we ate with a glass of wine while we sat by the van and watched the sun slide in to the sea.

As if this wasn't all perfect enough, the campsite has an indoor swimming pool so we went for an evening swim which is a really great thing to do after a lot of walking and gives you that lovely, floppy feeling that makes you just want to pour yourself in to bed and have one of those deep, deep sleeps that means you wake up looking 10 years younger (I wish!).

Liz returned to her caravan and I felt so privileged to have had such a wonderful day. To me, days like this are part of what I think people are talking about when they want to get a campervan so that they can *'live the dream'*. I'm always amazed at how many people are so enthusiastic when I tell them about our campervan and some of the adventures we have had in him. They confess that they would like to *'live the dream'* as well but think that they can't afford it and I hope that writing about our journey with Trev-the-Prev can show them that it can be done on a small budget too.

I must admit, I still get childishly excited when we pack up the van, jump in it and drive off on a trip. Every time! And I hope you do too and that it never leaves us.

Just One Glitch in Our Perfect Day...

There was just one negative thing that happened on that perfect day although, in a way, it has been a gift to me as it has helped me to understand and empathise with something that I would never have experienced otherwise.

When I first arrived at the campsite by myself several of the other campers talked to me and we had some nice chats and I even felt a slighted protective feeling from some of the couples there, which was nice. However, this seemed to change after Liz had visited and, although they were still polite, they were quite distant. This puzzled me for a bit and then I realised that they thought Liz and I were partners. We have been friends for over 25 years and are very comfortable together so I guess people just assumed that we were in a relationship.

Their new behaviour did feel a bit uncomfortable and it made me realise that this is what gay people probably experience a lot of the time which seems such a shame. Come on world, please stop this behaviour and treat people according to their kindness and their goodness and nothing else.

THE RECIPE:

Marvo Cheese on Toast

This is a no-cook open sandwich that includes marmite and avocado (hence Marvo). I know it sounds a bit of a quirky combo but these flavours all do a wonderful dance together. I appreciate that some people don't like Marmite and may need therapy at just the thought of it but you can leave that out – it's still tasty.

BREAD FOR TOASTING

A RIPE AVOCADO

PHILADELPHIA CREAM CHEESE

MARMITE

BALSAMIC GLAZE

How to Make

Toast the bread. If you don't have a toaster or a grill just pan fry it in a dry frying pan

Spread a thin layer of Marmite on the toast

Spread a generous layer of the cream cheese on the Marmite

Lay slices of avocado on top of the cream cheese

Drizzle and swirl a little balsamic glaze on top of the avocado

So What Sort of Camper Are

You...?

'Going camping' can mean so many different things today, from pitching on the side of a wind-blown hill in a tent the size of a tea-bag, glamping in a super-cosy shepherd's hut to spending a luxurious weekend in an RV fit for a celebrity. The world of camping is so much more than throwing up a heavy canvas tent as it would have been 20 years ago. Now, camping is quite trendy and I think that has partly come about because of the rise of the 'staycation' – staying in your own country to holiday rather than flying abroad. Since the economic crash in 2008 and with the rise of terrorist activity people either can't afford to go abroad or just don't want to risk it. So, what better way to make your staycation fun (and relatively inexpensive) than to go camping.

One of the most popular types of camping now is the small campervan and this is growing all the time and I just love all the different and creative ways people are converting anything from a regular car to an old bus into camping vehicles. In fact, I have to admit to being slightly addicted to Pinterest now as we are designing our own conversion (in a Vauxhall Vivaro) and I just love seeing what other people have done.

One of the most simple yet clever micro-campers that I have come across belonged to a middle-aged German couple I met on a campsite in Devon. They had been camping for 25 years (some of that with their 3 children) in a Volvo estate car which the husband had converted himself by putting a small 'bedroom' on the roof which would pop up out of a wooden, box-frame fitted to the roof bars. You enter the roof bedroom by climbing up the back of the vehicle. They had been camping in tents for some years but, this was difficult for their holidays in Norway as it is mainly rock there and you can't knock the pegs in so they decided it was time for a campervan. They wanted a small vehicle to be able to go down the narrow roads easily and their Volvo nano-camper is still going strong.

However, if you are going to buy or convert a campervan you first need to decide what sort of camper you are and I have come to the conclusion that there are five main camping styles in the campervan world:

1. Day Camping: where you just want a comfortable place to sit/make a cup of tea while you are out for the day

2. Week Camping: where you want to camp for up to a week for, say, a dozen times throughout each spring/summer/autumn and you need a fairly good bed, some inside seating and reasonable cooking facilities.

3. Month Camping: where you go on longer trips that take you away from home for a month to six months and in different climates. Now you want a proper bed, a roomy stand-up interior, some loo facilities, heating

and some decent seating. This type of camping is probably mostly done by the retired community.

4. Year Camping: Where you want to have a mega adventure and go off in the van for a year or two. Now you need everything you have in the Month Camping section plus a lot more storage. This is mainly done by free-spirit 20-somethings or intrepid young families.

5. Live-in camping: This is where you choose to live in your van as a permanent thing and so is not really camping but is a whole lifestyle in itself.

Naturally, everyone is different and some people are happy to go away for months in a week-style camper but I am just mentioning the ideal here.

Glyn and I are 'Week Campers' at the moment as Glyn works a standard Monday-Friday job so we are mainly limited to long weekends or a week throughout the year. With Trev-the-Prev being a micro-camper, we are also a bit limited by the seasons in this country as he doesn't have much interior. Of course, it would be lovely to take off for a few weeks to southern Spain in the winter (we just love Seville) but that would be a long trip and we don't have that much free time. Sigh! So, for now we are 'Week campers' but we hope to create a lifestyle in the future where we can work from anywhere with Wi-Fi and then we can be more nomadic.

But, from what I've seen, where a campervan or motorhome really comes in to its own is when you retire. A couple of our retired friends took off for 3 weeks to explore Scotland in their Nissan and had a magical time. They could have stayed longer if they had wanted to and its great to have the freedom to wander to your own rhythm.

43

Mind & Body Transition

I don't know about you, but I find that it takes a good day and a half to click in to campervan mode when you first set off on your adventure. It really is a mind and body transition and I can understand why people who have been away for a few months find it quite difficult to transition back to living in a house again. I sometimes find it really frustrating to have to come home at the end of a long weekend as I am just getting in the swing of it and feeling quite mellow after a few deep sleeps in the van. I also find that you start to get what I call the 'golden' look. I notice that people who spend regular time outside seem to get a golden look to their skin, it's not exactly a tan but a sort of healthy glow.

When I was doing a cooking demo at one of the Motorhome shows I got to talk to some of the stall-holders there. On one of the stands they had a member of staff who hadn't been to a motorhome show before and she was amazed at all the senior people that she was meeting. She said that she had never met so many retired people who had such a zest for life and who seemed so happy. So, camping seems to be healthy for you on the inside as well as the outside.

So what sort of camper are you? Are you like us, frustrated Month-Campers who have to be happy with Week-Camping for the moment. Are you like many of the free-spirited twenty-something couples I see on Instagram who are Year-Campers, travelling around the world in their van. Or have you gone the whole way and now live in your van (apparently quite a few students are doing this now to avoid having so much massive debt to pay back at the end of their courses)?

Whichever style of camping you are doing at the moment, you will be living the dream in your own way and that is a life-enhancing thing.

THE RECIPE:

Creamy Mustard Chicken

1 SMALL LEEK, SLICED

HALF A PACK OF GREEN BEANS, CHOPPED IN TO 1" LENGTHS

2 CHICKEN BREASTS CUT IN TO 2" STRIPS

100ML DOUBLE CREAM

1 TBSP COARSE GRAIN MUSTARD

1 TSP HORSERADISH SAUCE

1 TBSP RUNNY HONEY

SALT AND PEPPER TO TASTE

How to Cook

Fry leeks and beans in a little oil. Add a splash of water if necessary. Set aside.

In the same pan (unwashed) cook the chicken strips until nicely browned

Return the veg to the pan and add the cream

Sit in the mustard, horseradish sauce and honey and simmer gently for about 5 minutes

Serve with mashed potato or on rice.

Campervan Tip No 5: Take some flip-flops (or other plastic shoes) that you can wear in the shower. Makes the whole showering experience a lot easier and, sometimes, more hygienic.

How to 'Do' Cities...

One of the deep joys of owning a campervan is that you get to spend time out in Nature. You wake up to the sound of birdsong, breathe fresh air and really get to know the sky and landscape. You may even sit on a beach and eat your supper while you watch the sun go down. Bliss! But it is also possible to use your campervan to have a city break now and then and these can be great fun too, especially when the weather isn't so good. Let me tell you about one of our city breaks and how to 'do' a city when you are camping.

BoHo Brighton

It was late summer and Glyn and I had planned a long weekend away to the Brecon Beacons in Wales. I am a little bit in love with Brecon and the landscape there and it is definitely near the top of our list of places to get to know well. However, as the weekend approached, the weather forecast got worse and worse and we realised that it just wasn't realistic to go for a couple days walking in the Welsh hills that weekend but no way was I going to give up my time out vanning.

So, we did an online scan of the UK and what the weather was going to be like for the weekend and most of it was not good news but the south coast looked OK, especially Brighton. So, back on to Google and it wasn't long before we'd booked a campsite just outside of the city, packed the van and took off south.

I wasn't quite sure what to expect from Brighton as the last time I visited it was back in the early nineties when, not only was I very different, I imagine Brighton was different too and I don't really have that much memory of it. I knew that it was a lively place and has the nickname 'London-by-the-Sea' so guessed it would make for an interesting couple of days.

There aren't that many campsites right next to Brighton but there are a few along the coast and we found one that was OK but not brilliant but it would do for a couple of nights and we were going to be out all day anyway.

We decided that no way were we going to drive in to Brighton as, not only is it stressful trying to find parking in a city you don't know, you will probably have to take out a second mortgage! So, we drove to the park-and-ride and hopped on the bus making sure that we got the front seat at the top of the bus (yes, my inner five-year-old had taken over at the point). I love travelling at the top of a bus as you get to see the things you wouldn't normally see and it's great for having a nosy in to people's houses and gardens (admit it, we all do it if we can). House-watching in Brighton is a real sport as the houses there are pretty spectacular (I think we must have been driving down Millionaire's row) and it was fun to gasp at them and decide which ones we really liked and which ones were less than tasteful.

We got off in the middle of town and got on to Google maps on our phones to see where we were. I don't know about you but I love that feeling of landing in the middle of a new place and finding out where you are and where you want to go – just feels really free and exciting. We decided it was time for coffee so had a wander around the cute shops in the The Lanes and found a gorgeous artisan coffee shop with serious, barista coffee and chocolate brownies to die for (yes Glyn and I are unashamed coffee geeks). It gave us a chance to sit and plan the day a little and decided that the following were on the list to do:

1. See the Brighton Pavilion
2. Do a bit of shopping (OK that was my one)
3. Have a walk by the beach
4. Find a quirky place for lunch

We thought that would be enough for a general plan and we would do 'sponnys' (what my New Zealand friend calls anything spontaneous) if we found something more interesting along the way.

Brighton is a little bit surreal. In places you do really feel like you are walking through central London as the buildings and roads look very similar except that you can hear seagulls and smell the sea. One of the most surreal parts of the city is The Royal Pavilion, a beautiful maharishi-style building that looks like it should be in Mumbai. It really is very exotic and was built in 1787 as a seaside pleasure palace for King George IV, and it mixes Regency grandeur with the visual style of India and China.

Shop 'til You Drop

After this it was time to shop, and ladies, this is shopping heaven. In fact, it would be a sin not to shop while you are there. I won't bore you with the details of my shopping quest but I just have to tell you about a quirky, kitchen gadget that we bought there. As fate would have it, we came across the most gorgeous, huge and gadget-soaked kitchen shop that I have ever seen and I have to admit I went quite weak at the knees. I could happily have bought half the place but my favourite buy was the unusual chocolate sprinkler we got for our coffees. It's a little black and white cow and when you turn her upside down and shake her she moos! As I write this I realise that it sounds quite bizarre but when in Brighton....

Our late lunch was at a funky American Diner where they served stuffed beef burgers. Mine had blue cheese and fried onions in the middle and it works really well so it is something that I like to do for our campervan meals now, too. It's really easy. When you form up your burger just make a thumb-print hole in the middle and poke a little cheese and anything else you fancy in to the middle and then close it up and cook as normal.

After lunch it was time for a walk along the seafront and as the weather was fantastic (strange that it can be so different on such a small island) everybody was out at the beach and there was a really lively atmosphere – lots of music, art, food and people just having a good time.

As the day started to close and the legs started to get tired we made our way back to the city and the park-and-ride bus stop and we were relieved to have a bit of a sit down as it took us back to Trev in the car park. I don't think I could live in Brighton (even if we did win the lottery) but it was really good fun for a day.

Since then we have done similar city breaks in York and London and would recommend both and we plan to do many more as each city has a different personality and it is great to have a chance to just wander and explore.

My Checklist for Doing a City Break

1. Pick a weekend when the weather isn't too good so that you are not walking around the streets wishing you were on the beach or in the hills to make the most of the great weather.

2. Do an internet reccie. Check out the city to get a general feel of it and what you might like to do there and also to find and book a campsite. Usually there are not many campsites around a big city so you may want to make sure that you have something reasonable secured before you get there unless you are going wild.

3. Find out where the park-and-rides are and park there for the day. Make sure that you sit at the top of the bus ☺

4. Once you get to the city find a coffee shop and sit and check out the city on Google maps to see where everything is. You can also ask your barista any questions about the city and we have got some really good information this way.

5. If there is one close, go to the Tourist Information and get a city map and ask the lovely people there about anything special going on or what is good to see. We did this when we went to York and found out about a brilliant Ghost Walk tour that takes you around the city in the evening. We learned a lot about the amazing history there on the tour and had a lot of fun too.

6. Pick somewhere unusual for lunch. In a city you often have lots of interesting cafes/restaurants that you wouldn't see anywhere else so don't play it safe – try something new.

7. If shopping is in your soul, make sure that you build in at least a little time for some shopping.

8. Be spontaneous and go with it if you come across something interesting that you weren't expecting.

9. Plan a chilled evening by the van as you will probably want to just relax and fall in to bed.

THE RECIPE:

Stuffed Sliders

Sliders are just small burgers and go really well in a bun. You can play around with different cheeses and I really like adding a bit of blue cheese sometimes.

500gms MINCED BEEF

2-3 STRIPS OF BACON CHOPPED INTO SMALL PIECES

½ CUP GRATED CHEDDAR

1 TEASPOON WORCESTERSHIRE SAUCE

1 TEASPOON MUSTARD

SALT AND PEPPER TO TASTE

LETTUCE TOMATO, RED ONION, AVOCADO FOR TOPPINGS

BURGER BUNS

How to Make

Place the beef in a bowl, and add the worcestershire sauce, mustard, and a few dashes of salt and pepper, mix thoroughly

Place the chopped bacon in a pan and saute over medium-high until crispy. Remove the bacon once it is done and let it cool

Place the cheese and bacon pieces in a bowl and mix so they are distributed evenly.

With your hands, make bacon cheese balls about ½" to ¾".

Form 2" minced beef patties and use your finger to poke a hole in the middle of one side, but not all the way through. Insert a cheese and bacon ball and cover the hole up completely.

Grill, pan-fry or barbeque the stuffed patties on medium-high until they are cooked through.

Top your sliders with condiments and toppings and enjoy!

Finding Your Soul Home…

As you travel around the country (or countries) in your campervan do you find that, every now and then, you come across a place that just feels like 'home'? I don't mean that it looks like where you live, in fact it might be completely the opposite, but it touches your soul so deeply that you have to return to it again and again. I call it your Soul Home.

Our Soul Home at the moment is Dartmoor National Park in Devon, a large are of open moorlands and deep river valleys, with a rich history and rare wildlife. We have had many trips there in Trev-the-Prev including going wild at one our favourite spots which we discovered by accident on a warm summer's night.

Glyn and I had booked a weekend camping at one of our favourite sites on the west side of the moor near Tavistock (see below) but we planned to go wild on the Friday night as Glyn couldn't get time off work so we had to travel down later in the evening and there was no point in paying for a site for that night. We had a land ranger map of the moor (please do not go wandering around the moor without a map, it can be very disorientating) so we were just going to drive and pick a place to park up on the moor somewhere. That was the theory.

That night was one of those balmy, summer evenings that just feel delicious and I think everybody was heading down to the west country for the weekend. The M5 motorway was packed and we were still crawling along it at 10pm but it didn't seem to matter as there was a real party atmosphere there. When we stopped at the service station people were still walking around in shorts and flip flops, laughing and relaxed, and it felt like the whole world was on holiday.

The problem was that this meant that we arrived at the moor around midnight and were driving around in the dark trying to find a spot to park. The moor is very eerie at night (love it!) and we didn't really have any idea where we were going to end up but in the end, we found a spot in the woods by a river bridge and we tucked ourselves in there.

Strange Light Show

We jumped in to bed and were quickly asleep (quick tip: if you are going to arrive somewhere late have the bed already made up so you don't have to do it when you're tired). However, a couple of hours later we woke up with a sense that something weird was going on. We try and black out our sleeping area as we don't want to be woken up with the light at 5am but, even through the cracks, we could see that there was some strange sort of light show going on outside. We opened the door and looked out and could see that the sky was filled with white flashing lights that were pulsating, almost as bright as a football stadium. I did wonder if the army were doing some sort of military exercise in the middle of the night (a large part of Dartmoor is owned by the army) but there was absolutely no sound. This went on for a while and Glyn and I decide not to worry about it and went back to sleep (it could have been aliens landing and taking over the world but we were pretty shattered by then).

"Stress is caused from not camping enough."

The next day we found out what it was. Apparently, there had been a major storm with sheet lightning in that area and gale force winds. Why there was no thunder with our lightning I don't know but we had pretty much missed the whole thing and were so glad that we had parked up in our cosy little wood and not on one the more exposed areas of the moor (of which there are many).

It was also a deep joy to get up in the morning and finally see where we were parked which was absolutely gorgeous – one of the very pretty little rivers that run through the moor in what I call a faerie wood. We had a quick breakfast and a little walk in the wood before packing up and driving across the moor to our campsite, but I will never forget that night and how it felt to be looked after by our special woods. I know this all sounds a bit fanciful but you do start to feel the magic when you are on Dartmoor and I think this is one of the reasons why so many people are drawn to it, as well as it's rugged beauty.

Glyn and I particularly love all the amazing stone structures there – some are natural, like the tors, and others are made by ancient man, like the stone circles. The tors are huge structures of natural granite that crystalised there around 280 million years ago, but they feel like some sort of Inca temple when you stand beside them and it's hard to believe that nature has created it. Some of them even have what are known as hanging stones where a huge, multi-tonne stone seems to balance on top of another and looks as though it could topple off at any moment (they don't, I have tried it of course).

There are also many stone circles and stone rows that would have been built by Neolithic/Bronze age man and, to be honest, I don't think anyone really knows why they built them but they are incredible feats of engineering for people who still used deer antlers as tools.

One of our favourite stone circles is Scorhill Stone circle near Gidleigh on the east side of the moor. As you sit in the circle and look around you can only see moor, trees and sky, all signs of civilisation have gone. It is totally wild.

Soul Name

In fact, I think 'WILD' is the soul name of Dartmoor. I can't remember where I read this but, the author said that every place has its own personality that can be summed up in one word (its soul name as I call it). For example, Barcelona (another one of my soul homes) has the soul name 'EXPRESSION'. For me Brighton, one of our city breaks, has the soul name 'BOHEMIAN' and Oxford, where I used to live, has the soul name 'LEARNED'. I don't think you need to be a psychologist to work out that the places that you are drawn to and their soul qualities are probably similar to the qualities that you carry too. So, I suppose that makes me WILD, EXPRESSIVE, BOHEMIAN and LEARNED. I can live with that!

Perhaps when you are traveling around in your camper and come across a place that feels like a soul home you could decide what its soul name is. Maybe you might like to think what part of you also has that quality and celebrate that too.

THE RECIPE:

Spicy Bean Tacos

Our favourite campsite on Dartmoor is the Caravan & Camping Club Tavistock site and I did a little cooking demo on one of our visits there. I cooked one of our favourite, quick and easy, Tex-Mex style camping meals: Spicy Black Bean Tacos.

BLACK BEANS (2 X 230G PACKETS OR TINS), DRAINED

1 SMALL ONION FINELY CHOPPED

2 CLOVES OF GARLIC, MINCED

1 TUBE OF SQUEEZY TOMATO SALSA OR A CARTON OF PASSATA

2 TSPS CUMIN POWDER

1/2 TSP CHILLI POWDER (OR MORE IF YOU LIKE IT HOT)

1 TBSPS RUNNY HONEY

2 TBSPS PHILADELPHIA CHEESE

1/2 TSP SALT

How to Cook

Add 2 tbsps olive oil to a frying pan on medium heat

Add the onion and garlic and fry until soft

Add the black beans, tomato salsa and cook for 2-3 minutes adding a little water if it is too thick

Add the cumin and chilli powders and stir well

Add the honey, Philadelphia cheese and salt and let it cook for another minute or so

Serve in soft tacos with some Avocado Crema (See recipe in 'Why am I a Lazy Cook') and a little shredded lettuce. It's also good cooked in a tortilla with a little grated cheddar

Nature Nurture...

For me, one of the best things about camping is that you get to reconnect with Nature and remember what it feels like to be outdoors. Most of us spend so much time inside four walls, whether that is at home or at the office, and we lose touch with the natural world. This is not good.

Spending time in Nature is really important for our health (and our sanity). How good do you feel when you have spent a day by the ocean, walking on the beach and swimming in the sea (OK, having to remove sand from nearly every bodily crevice isn't so good, but it's a small price to pay I think).

Did you know that one of the reasons we feel so good when we are at the beach is because we are usually walking barefoot on the sand or in the sea and we are 'earthing'. Earthing happens when we walk on the earth barefoot (as we were meant to do) and we receive electrons from the ground through our feet. Shoes made from synthetic materials cut us off from this. These electrons are really important for our health, especially in the digital age when we are surrounded by electronic equipment that gives off positive ions. When we are grounded this way we sleep better, our immune system works better, we have more energy, our mood improves and we are just healthier in every way. I think this is one of the reasons that we often feel so deliciously relaxed after a day at the beach. So being out in Nature really does nurture us, not just on the soul level but also in very physical ways.

But, for me, one of the greatest joys of being in the natural world is seeing the wildlife.

Yay, Dolphins!

One particularly magical moment with wildlife happened on a lovely sunny day in Wales when we were eating lunch outside a harbourside pub in New Quay. This is not the famous surfing Newquay on the Cornish coast, but a little seaside town on the mid-west coast of Ceredigion (Cardiganshire in English). I think Ceredigion is my favourite county in Wales as it feels unspoilt and I think is one of those places that is beautiful in a gentle way and I always feel a longing to return when we come home from there.

The beaches around New Quay form a golden arc around a pretty bay (Cardigan Bay) and it is possible to see bottlenose dolphins there at certain times of the year, usually June to October, and there is even a local boat that will take you out on dolphin spotting trips. I fell in love with dolphins many years ago on a holiday to La Gomera, one of the lesser known islands in the Canaries. La Gomera is just stunning and its reputation for being a part of the lost city of Atlantis is justly deserved. My friend Liz and I have spent a few gorgeous Februarys there to escape the British winter and we always end up having brilliant adventures. One was being taken out dolphin spotting in a small boat by one of the local fishermen who offers occasional trips. Not only did we see pilot whales, which have the most serene energy about them, we were also visited by around 100 spotted dolphins who just whizzed around the boat obviously finding us interesting. You just cannot help smiling when dolphins are around as they are so playful and clearly having a lot of fun. After about 10 minutes they obviously had business elsewhere and, in complete synchronicity, shot-off in to the distance.

> "There is no wi-fi in the forest but I promise
>
> you will find a better connection."

The dolphins at New Quay come in to the bay on most days in the summer, mainly to feed on fish like bass, salmon and mackerel, although they do grub about on the sea bed and eat whatever they can find. The pub where we were having lunch is slightly up the hill so you get a good overall view of the bay and this day, the pod of dolphins came in to feed and it was really special as they had a baby with them. At one point, one of the dolphins must have seen some fish as it shot across the bay like a torpedo and I was shocked at the speed of it. But I will always remember this as a privileged moment as it was so lovely to sit and eat good food, in a beautiful location watching dolphins play. Doesn't get much better than that!

Campsite Robin

Of course, lovely nature moments don't always have to be with something as exotic as dolphins, I often really enjoy having a chat with the campsite robin. I don't know about you but, virtually every campsite we go to has a cheeky robin that comes around the back of the van in the morning hoping for some toast crumbs. Sometimes they are amazingly tame and come right up to your feet while you are eating as I guess they are born there and humans are just part of the landscape. It is also lovely to hear their song as you emerge from the van and one of the best parts of campervan life is sitting outside on a blue-sky morning, having a serious cooked breakfast (*Ranch Beans,* see below), listening to the birds and planning the day ahead, not forgetting to spill a few crumbs for Mr Robin, of course.

Psycho Seagull

Unfortunately, not all birds are as friendly as Mr Robin, some of them are positively psychopathic. I have experienced this first hand at one of the seaside towns we visited a couple of years ago (I can't remember which one, it was probably the concussion).

I had gone off to do a bit of shopping on the front by myself and I was feeling a bit peckish so decided to eat one of the rice cakes that I carry in my handbag for such occasions (yes, I do try to keep it healthy although I think this one may have had a layer of chocolate on it). As I walked along eating my rice cake I suddenly felt a big whack to the back of my head and found myself staring into the demonic eyes of a seagull that was trying to take my rice cake out of my hand! These birds are huge when you see them up-close and they have very sharp beaks but, on principle, he was not getting my rice cake. We continued to wrestle (The Camper Cookie does not surrender food without a fight) and, even though he had clearly had commando training, I eventually won and he gave up. But, then, he had the nerve, THE NERVE, to plop down a few feet in front of me and look at me sweetly, clearly waiting for me to feed him! I was still a bit stunned and I think I just said "Sod off" and walked away but the back of my head hurt for quite a while.

This has made me a bit cautious of eating on the sea front when seagulls are around as, in a lot of seaside towns, people have fed the gulls and they have now become food-muggers. From what I have seen, they tend to be stealth bombers and prefer to swoop in from the side or when you are not looking so, when you are eating your fish & chips from a bag sitting on the sea wall, keep an eye out for psycho seagulls and stare them down if they look your way.

THE RECIPE:

Ranch Beans

If you are barbequeing some sausages for your evening meal, add a couple extra and keep in the fridge for breakfast the next day or day after to have in this Ranch Beans recipe.

415 gms CAN OF BAKED BEANS

2-3 COOKED SAUSAGES CHOPPED IN TO SMALL PIECES AND/OR 3 RASHERS OF COOKED BACON CHOPPED IN TO PIECES

1TBSP BARBEQUE SAUCE OF YOUR CHOICE

How to Make

Put the beans in a saucepan

Add the sausage and/or bacon pieces

Add the barbeque sauce and stir

Heat on a medium heat and serve with some crusty bread and butter

For a veggie version, you could pan fry some mushrooms and add these to the beans.

Some People are Just Plain 'Difficult'...

Most of the people you meet on a campsite are great and it is fun talking about each other's vans and places that you have visited but, just every now and then, you come across 'difficult' people (I'm being polite there).

This happened when we stayed on one of our favourite campsites in Dorset on the coast near Bridport. At Highland's End you can park on pitches that are right on the cliffs and you have the most amazing sea views and Glyn and I had parked Trev on one of the best pitches nearest the sea. At Highlands, they don't give you a specific number you just go and park on an empty gravel plot. Unfortunately, this can cause a problem when you go off for the day and want to come back to your previous pitch. We didn't have a driveaway awning at that time but we did put up our utility tent where we store the table, chairs and general stuff when we drive off for the day so it was pretty clear that this pitch was occupied.

However, when we came back that evening there was a motorhome parked on our pitch even though there were plenty of other empty pitches around although not with the great views that our one had. A middle-aged couple were sitting next to the vehicle so we drove over to them and politely explained that this was our pitch and they had parked on it by mistake and could they please move. They muttered something which we took to be a grumpy agreement so we went and sat in our van ready to drive on as they moved but nothing happened. They were a South African couple and I was a bit surprised by this as nearly all of the South African people I have ever met have been delightful and usually have lovely manners.

We are having a Braai!

However, our couple were clearly digging in. We went and spoke to them again and pointed out our utility tent and that if we went to another plot we would have to move all our stuff and that wasn't reasonable but, by this time, they were getting shirty and the woman shrieked "We are having a braai!". I got the impression that she expected me to be thrown by the word 'braai' (South African for barbeque) but having had many braais in South Africa myself that didn't work.

Many years ago, I spent three months back-packing around Africa (with my then partner) which included a month in South Africa, a country that I fell passionately in love with despite the troubles there. This was in the days just before Nelson Mandela was released so apartheid was still evident and I was once politely told off by an Afrikaans man when I went in to the 'wrong' ladies loo at a garage. I hadn't noticed that there were two ladies' loos, one with a white lady figure above it and the other with a black lady sign and I had gone in to the one with the black lady without even noticing, not being used to a choice of toilets. When he heard my English accent, he apologised but said that this was something we needed to be aware of while we were there.

We had stopped at the garage to fill up the classic VW campervan that we had hired for the week (or Kombi as they call them there). Our camper was a bright orange colour so we called it 'The Naartjie' which is a gorgeously juicy tangerine-like fruit that is popular in South Africa. We had the most amazing time driving around what is a beautiful country and it is very different camping there. For a start, you don't just wander off in to the bush for a pee if you need one as you could end up being somebody's dinner (to put it bluntly, you just pee at the back of the van). Also, we once had to stop for some time on the dirt road that we were driving on to let a python cross the road. At one point his head was in the bushes on one side while his tail was still in the bushes on the other which gives you an idea of the size of him. We weren't going to argue.

Out there you can also camp inside the national parks and we camped in the Kruger National Park for a couple of nights. As you can imagine, the campsites are surrounded by very high fencing and you can sit by your van at dusk and listen to the lions roaring as they get ready to go hunting. If you've never heard that sound before it is impossible to really describe how it feels but it goes right through you on some primal level and every cell in your body quakes with fear.

Cheeky Monkey

I also had a funny moment with some of the wildlife when we were camping next to one of the lakes up in the north east of the country (you know, the ones which are full of flamingos – stunning!) These campsites aren't fenced and I was cooking up one of my famous chicken stews for supper on a table just next to the van. I had just peeled a large onion ready to chop it up for the stew and I turned to go back in to the van to find a knife when, suddenly, a monkey rushed out of the bushes, grabbed the onion off the table and ran off with it. He'd clearly been watching me from the bushes and picked his moment. I tried to be annoyed but it was quite funny and I smiled trying to imagine his face when he bit in to it. I love Africa!

Anyway, back to Dorset...LOL. It's true our South African couple did have a very small portable barbeque that could have easily been carried but were obviously using it as an excuse. The lady then said, "You don't expect us to move the braai" and I explained that that was exactly what we expected them to do but by now they were ignoring us and clearly any negotiations were over.

Luckily the campsite managers were still on site so we went and spoke to them and, from their reaction, it was clearly not the first time that they had had to sort out something like this and they asked us to drive out of sight to avoid more conflict and let them deal with it.

After about 10 minutes they came back to us and said that the people were moving and to give them a few more minutes to drive to another pitch which they did. The site managers said that it was very obvious that that pitch was occupied because of the utility tent but the other couple had taken it because they wanted the better view.

The site managers also suggested something that we have found to be useful when camping at other sites where the pitches are not numbered. They said it would be worth getting a marker that we could stick in the middle of the gravel or grass when we drive off in the daytime to show that the pitch was taken. Apparently, some people buy an extra number plate of their vehicle and put it on a stick so that they can use it wherever they go and it is then very clear which vehicle is parked there. As we later learned, Highland's End do let people borrow a marker from the office (for a deposit which is returned) to try and stop this happening but we didn't know that at the time. However, they said that it probably wouldn't have stopped people like our intruders as they were clearly intent on having that pitch no matter what. The strange thing was, the South African couple were only staying overnight so it makes you wonder was it really necessary to invade somebody else's pitch for just one night? I will just never understand some people!

Anyway, I'm sure that you also have some stories of painful people at some of the campsites that you have stayed at but I guess that difficult people are just part of life and we don't stop being human just because we are camping. Luckily, I find that most campers are interesting, adventurous and happy people so maybe we just have to take the rough with the smooth and put it down to experience.

THE RECIPE:

Hearty Chicken Stew

This is a one-pot recipe that I make a lot at home too and it is one of those comfort dishes that is great for a cold night or when you just need a 'food-cuddle'. You can play around with the ingredients depending on what veg you have (I also add frozen peas when we are at home but as we don't have a freezer in the van this doesn't happen when we are camping).

I LARGE POTATO (SKIN-ON, CUT IN TO MOUTH-SIZED PIECES)

SOME ROOT VEG E.G. CARROT, TURNIP, SWEDE (CUT IN TO MOUTH-SIZED PIECES)

HALF A 250g BOX OF MUSHROOMS (SLICED)

A SMALL ONION (CHOPPED)

2 TBSPS. TOMATO PUREE

1 TSP MARMITE (OPTIONAL)

HALF A STOCK CUBE

A SMALL CAN (200g) OF BAKED BEANS (THESE DISAPPEAR AS YOU COOK IT)

AND FOR THE SECRET INGREDIENT... A TBSP. OF SMOOTH, PEANUT BUTTER (STRANGE BUT TRUE!)

1 TSP OF DRIED HERBS OF YOUR CHOICE E.G. THYME, SAGE, OREGANO, ROSEMARY AND, INTERESTINGLY, A TSP OR GARAM MASALA ALSO DOES WONDERS FOR THE FLAVOUR.

2 BREASTS OF CHICKEN (CUT IN TO MOUTH-SIZED PIECES)

How to Cook

Take a large saucepan and fill to about a third full of water. Add the stock cube and tomato puree and stir

Add the chopped potato, onions and root veg and cook for around 10 minutes

Add the herbs and spices, marmite, baked beans and the peanut butter and stir. Also add the mushroom and chicken pieces (and if you have a freezer it is nice to add frozen peas at this point)

Cook for another 5-10 minutes, adding any extra water if necessary, until you are sure that the chicken is cooked through. Serve

Serve in large bowls and sprinkle with a little grated, mature cheddar. Lovely with crusty bread for dipping in the tasty soup.

Having a Theme is Fun...

Sometimes, when you go camping, it is more fun if you have a 'theme' for the trip or even a have a theme for your whole camping year.

Glyn and I have an on-going camping theme that is in the background of most of our trips and that is to visit any ancient sacred sites in the area. I have long been fascinated by sacred sites, like long barrows, stone circles, standing stones and ancient churches, and in Britain we are lucky to have so many. I live in Wiltshire which is home to Stonehenge and to Avebury stone circles as well as being regularly covered in crop circles so it would be a bit rude not to be a little bit interested. Virtually everywhere you go in this country, you can bet that there is a sacred site not too far away.

Not only does the history and the mystery of these places intrigue me, if you visit these sites you will often find that it takes you to some gorgeous landscape that you wouldn't normally ever see and you often get a nice walk out of it, too.

Glyn and I are totally in love with Dartmoor in Devon and this is virtually a theme park for sacred sites. If you look on an ordinance survey map of the area you can see many of them marked and it is often fun to plan a walk to visit that particular stone row, megalith or tor. One of our favourite sacred places on Dartmoor is Scorhill stone circle on the east side. You have to walk a little way on to the moor to find it but it is well worth it especially as it is hidden in a dip and you start to think you've lost it and then suddenly, like magic, it appears in front of you. As you stand there you are completely surrounded by moor and all signs of the 21st century have disappeared which can feel a bit scary at first and then it is just plain thrilling. It also gives you an idea of what life must have been like centuries ago and you really feel a connection to the land. However, you do have to be a bit careful on Dartmoor as it can be very disorientating, especially if the mist comes down, and always wear some warm layers as it is often colder than you think.

However, you don't have to be in the middle of a moor to find sacred sites. When we went on one of our city breaks to York we found a group of three absolutely massive standing stones nearby in Boroughbridge. They are called the Devil's Arrows and are literally on the edge of the village, about 200 metres from the A1(M) motorway, and stand over 20ft high (gulp!). These places, wonderfully, often have a mysterious legend attached to them. In this case it is said that, The Devil, irritated by some slight from the local people, threw the stones at the village from his place on a local hill. His poor aim, or maybe divine intervention, meant that the "arrows' fell short by a good mile. It is also claimed that walking 12 times around the stones anti-clockwise will raise the Devil. Don't think I really want to find out if that one works!

Given that these stone monuments were created in the Neolithic or early bronze age it makes you wonder how the people of the time ever managed to move them and build them with no serious equipment. I'm also intrigued as to why our ancestors went to all the trouble to create these places (which often link up on long-range alignments) but that is a whole other book in itself.

We have visited many sacred sites over the years and there are some yummy colour pictures in the gallery on my website, www.thecampercookie.com, if you fancy a visual feast.

Of course, you don't have to stick at just one theme – you can have 'parallel themes' too. Glyn and I, being coffee geeks, make it our mission to find the best coffee shop wherever we go and we often talk with wistful nostalgia about some of the special ones that we have found (sad I know but it keeps us happy). At one of the campsites that we stayed on near Dartmoor, they even had a lady bring her mobile coffee cart on to the site each morning so you could go and get a proper cappuccino to start your day. Great idea!

At the moment, we have **two new themes** which we will start in our 2018 camping year (and probably go beyond).

Theme 1: The RSPB

The first theme involves the RSPB (Royal Society for the Protection of Birds). I was in my local garden centre the other day and I had a great chat with a lady from the RSPB who had a stand there. I love my garden and Glyn and I are passionate about the huge amount of birdlife that come and visit us there (if I am not quick enough, the robin will sit on a perch outside the kitchen window and stare me down until I give them their breakfast) and it was nice to chat to someone so knowledgeable. She was also able to give me some advice on looking after the hedgehogs we have in the garden. It had been a very hot couple of weeks and one of our hedgehogs was wandering around the garden in the daytime looking a bit dazed and she advised me to give him a drink of water as they often get dehydrated in hot weather (please never give them milk, it is bad for them).

We didn't know it but the RSPB is not just for bird watchers as it covers all the wildlife in Britain so it is a good way to learn about our native creatures and, when you join, you get a directory of all their nature reserves around the country which you can visit. So, this is our plan: take off in the campervan to go and visit these interesting places, have lovely walks and learn more about our wildlife.

Theme No 2: Food Festivals

So, wildlife reserves are new theme number one. New theme number two is to visit a few more food festivals. We really enjoyed visiting the Abergavenny Food Festival weekend in 2017 and it has given us a taste (sorry for the pun) for more. We have also been to the food festival that they hold in Bristol Harbour a couple of times and we had a gorgeous day sitting around in the sun at the water's edge. I always learn something new, whether that is a cooking technique or a new foodie product. Of course, it also involves eating lots of yummy food and drinking stuff you would never normally try – and I surprised myself by how much I liked the toffee vodka we discovered there.

"KEEP CALM

and

GO CAMPING."

I am afraid that there is a bit if a story around me and vodka and, if you just mention the word to Glyn, he bursts out laughing. When I was doing some freelance accounts work, one of my clients was a Russian company who brings small groups over from Russia for a cultural experience of Britain. They are lovely people and invited us to one of their social evenings for some eats and drinks. We were treated to caviar and other Russian cuisine as well as, of course, Russian vodka specially brought over for us. I am not much of a drinker, usually only ever having a glass or two of wine with a meal or a Pimm's in the garden in the summer. I *never* drink vodka. But they gave me a glass of this obviously very special vodka so I felt it would be rude not to drink it. After I drank it I was feeling very thirsty and I spotted a bottle of water on the table so helped myself to a glass of it. To my horror it was the vodka (it was a clear bottle with no label) and they had seen me take it and were smiling at my enthusiasm so I just couldn't throw it away. I drank the vodka - all of it.

I don't remember much after that but Glyn said that I was extremely chatty and extrovert and I do remember having the hiccups at one point but it didn't seem to stop me from speaking (non-stop) in a loud voice to anyone and everyone. Normally when they see me I am in business mode and very sober (in both ways) but that night I seemed to be channelling my inner Patsy from

AbFab. It didn't seem to spoil the business relationship in any way (in fact I think they were quite impressed by my vodka keenness) and I think they just put it down to eccentric English behaviour (bless them) but I do squirm a bit when I think about it.

So, for me, high-octane vodka is now off limits, (Glyn tells people to lock up their vodka when we are visiting, cheeky bugger) but I must admit the odd toffee vodka (just one normal sized glass) is quite nice now and then.

Anyway, this is probably way too much information so back to the food festivals. Even if you are not a foodie like me, a day out at a food festival is good fun and here are a few that you might like to try:

- Abergavenny Food festival, Welsh Border (September)
- Bristol Harbour Food Festival (May)
- Ludlow Food Festival, Shropshire (September)
- The Big Feastival, Oxon (August)
- Loch Lomond Food & Drink Festival, Scotland (September)
- Aldeburgh Food & Drink Festival, Suffolk (September)
- Pommery Dorset Seafood Festival, Dorset (July)

Other Themes to Try

I also have a growing number of other themes that I would like to follow on our campervan holidays (I think I may need to just live in the van to squeeze them all in) and they are:

- Find some secret beaches
- Hire electric bikes and go exploring for the day
- Eat cream teas in beautiful gardens (Glyn is Mr Devon when it comes to cream teas; cream first and jam on top. I am Ms Cornwall; jam first and then cream on top which, of course, is the best way to do it!)

Perhaps you can think of some themes for your campervan trips in the future. If so, please do share on my website (www.thecampercookie.com) and inspire other people too.

THE RECIPE:

Super Refreshing Lime Quencher (ABSOLUTELY NO VODKA)

1 FRESH LIME

SOME LEMONADE OR SPARKLING WATER

1 TSP SUGAR (OR XYLITOL TO BE HEALTHIER)

A SPRIG OF MINT

How to Make

Roll the lime on a hard surface (to make it juicier) and then cut open and squeeze the juice in to a glass. Cut the rind in to slices.

Add the sugar and stir to dissolve

Add the lemonade or sparkling water

Add the sprig of mint and the lime rind slices. Enjoy.

This is so simple yet the most refreshing drink I have ever tasted.

Campervan Tip No 6: When you get up in the morning try and do a few dynamic warm-up exercises and stretches. Sleeping in a campervan bed and doing all the extra climbing in and out of the van can hurt your muscles if you don't take care of them.

Move it or Lose it...

One of the many benefits of owning a campervan is that it gets you outdoors doing sporty things that you might not normally do. For those of us that sit at a desk most of the week this can be a bit of a shock to the system but, what the heck, let's live dangerously.

Over the years, Trev-the-Prev has taken Glyn and I to some very great places where we were able to do our sports or try something completely new. We are both horse riders (Glyn learned to ride with the Life Guards in Knightsbridge, lucky boy) and we have had some wonderful rides out on Dartmoor. If you want to forget life's problems, just get on a horse and go galloping across a moor – it is impossible not to be ecstatic!

Having a van also means that you can just take off for a weekend if you have a course or workshop that you want to go to. Glyn does Aikido and his club were holding a one-day workshop down on the Dorset course (what's not to like) so we took Trev down for the weekend and, while Glyn was at his class, I went off walking along the beautiful coastal path there. I love walking with friends but there is something really special about walking on your own. You experience the landscape in a very different way, partly because you have to concentrate a bit more so you don't get lost, but also you sort of go in to your own special world and everything seems more beautiful and more intense. Of course, my day out had to start with a seriously good brunch at The Soulshine Café in Bridport which does gorgeous cake and coffee too and you can often see TV celebrities in there as quite a few of them have holiday homes in the area. I guess Dorset is the part of the West Country that is a reasonable commute from London.

Trying Something New

Going away camping has also encouraged us to try something that we wouldn't normally have thought about: exploring on electric bikes. Now, I know a lot of serious cyclists snort at the thought of an electric bike and, if you are the sort of person who could comfortably complete the Tour de France, it won't be for you but, if you don't have that level of fitness or you just want to enjoy seeing places, then an electric bike is a great alternative. It's also a myth that the bike does all the work for you like a moped does. On an electric bike you are still peddling, you just get a bit of help which makes a big difference on the hills and means that you can travel further than you would normally manage. Glyn has a good way of explaining what it is like to ride an electric bike – he says that it is similar to walking along the travellator (moving floor) at an airport; you are still walking but you get there faster and with less effort. I think that, on an electric bike or on a normal bike, you get to experience our beautiful countryside in a more intimate way that you would ever be able to do in a car or van.

Out first experience of electric bikes was when we hired some via a Groupon deal and had a cycling day out around the Cotswolds and got to see some of the pretty back roads we didn't even know existed. Of course, it was also necessary to stop at a gorgeous country pub with great views for lunch where we could re-charge our battery packs while we ate. We did a 30-mile round trip and, for people who don't normally cycle, didn't feel too sore the next day. Many bike hire places around the country now hire out electric bikes as well as normal pushbikes and, although it feels a little strange at first, you soon get used to riding them. Why not give it a go?

Another ourdoor-sy activity we got to try on a camping adventure was kayaking up the river in the beautiful Wye valley near the Welsh border. I just love the Wye valley as I think it is one of the most beautiful and gentle river valleys in the country and you pass atmospheric ruins such as Tintern Abbey which sit silently along its banks.

We hired one of those double kayaks, the type that the American Indians used to paddle, and I was at the front steering (God help us) and Glyn was at the back providing the muscle. It took us a little while to get the hang of it, I think I did steer us under some trees at one point, but you quickly learn to just close your eyes, duck and hang on and after a while we were effortlessly gliding along the river. When you quietly paddle along a river like this it's almost as though the wildlife accepts you and lets you into their world and you get to know nature in a way that you wouldn't do by just walking through it. The guide who came with us was very excited about spotting some otter scat (pooh) which didn't do a lot for me but I guess that, for somebody who is so connected to the river, it was exciting to know that the otters were near. We would like to try some sea kayaking on our campervan adventures next year and my hope is to see some seals up close.

"Home is where you park it."

So, what other wacky things have we tried on our camping trips? I sometimes buy Glyn a car driving experience for his birthday (Groupon, yet again, does some good deals) so we combine that with a camping weekend and, so far, he has driven: a stunt car, Jaguar F-type, Aston Martin Vantage and Ariel Atom (0-60 in 2.5 seconds). It means nothing to me, but Glyn tells me that you boys are probably drooling right now!

Wipeout!

Another thing that I think will be on our future 'to-do-while-camping' list is body boarding. Many years ago, when I was a lot younger and sports-fit, I tried a learn-to-surf day. I love being in the sea and have always thought that gliding effortlessly on a surfboard would feel serene and transcendental. I was wrong. It is really hard. I'm sure, like many sports, once you have mastered the skills, it must feel fantastic but all I can remember was spending a lot of time upside down in the water and swallowing a lot of it (when you get washed off the board like this it is called a Wipeout).

Our instructors gave us some tuition on the beach before we were allowed in the water and it seems to me that getting up on to a surf board is a big like doing a press-up on a jelly. However, I did manage to stand up on the board for a few seconds before falling off and swallowing yet more water. I seemed to be very good at getting to a kneeling position and surfing that way which I quite enjoyed so maybe I should adopt that as my speciality (I realise that you serious surf dudes probably find this slightly ridiculous, and why wouldn't you?).

However, it has given me a greater respect for the sport and I appreciate the skill and effort that goes in to the seemingly effortless appearance of the people that do surf well. I was also amazed at how physically challenging it is, not just the surfing itself but having to keep swimming out past the waves. When we stopped for lunch on my course, several of the extremely fit 20-something men were actually shaking, not with the cold but because they had completely depleted their glucose levels. Surfers really are the gymnasts of the sea.

But, from that day I now know two things: surfing people are interesting, soulful people and, I love body boarding! For those who are not familiar, body boarding is like surfing except you don't stand up, you lie face down on the board as you cruise in on a wave. It feels a lot faster and more dramatic than it looks and I find I have to stop myself from going 'Wheee' as I glide in (so not cool, I know). I guess the next mission is to go and find a wet-suit that will fit without looking like there are actually three people inside of it. Devon coast, here we come!

THE RECIPE:

Oaty Energy Balls

If you are going to do sporty things when you are out in the campervan you are going to need to keep your energy up and one of the easiest and tastiest ways to do this is to make some energy balls that you can eat as a snack when you feel your energy dropping. If you are going away for just a few days, you can make these before you go but remember to keep them in the fridge

1 CUP ROLLED OATS

1/2 CUP PEANUT BUTTER

1/4 CUP HONEY

1/4 CUP SHREDDED COCONUT

1/4 CUP CHOCOLATE CHIPS

2 TABLESPOONS GROUND FLAXSEEDS (OR VANILLA PROTEIN POWDER)

1 TEASPOON VANILLA

 PINCH OF SEA SALT

How to Make

Put all ingredients in a large bowl and stir together well to combine.

Place bowl of "dough" in the fridge for 30 minutes to an hour so it can set up.

Bring dough out of the fridge and roll into balls about 1 Tablespoon in size.

Store in a covered container in the fridge.

Keep on Living the Dream…

Well, I hope you have enjoyed spending a little time with us on our adventures in Trev-the-Prev and hopefully it has given you a few more ideas for things that you can try on your campervan adventures, too. However, always avoid ninja seagulls, be careful where you choose to wild park and keep away from the vodka.

Our time with Trev is now coming to an end and we are now converting a Vauxhall Vivaro SWB called 'Big Red'. No doubt we will be having more quirky adventures in him too so watch out for – **'Adventures of a Lazy Campervan Cook 2'**

Recipe Index

About the Author

Summer Bourne

Summer grew up in London and has followed many different careers from technical copywriting through to being a house therapist (somebody who can 'cure' unhealthy houses).

However, she has always been passionate about natural health and cooking good food was an essential part of that.

Her passion for nutritious food also came out of what she learned when she cured herself of Chronic Fatigue Syndrome as nutrition was a key part of that process.

So, when Summer and her partner Glyn got their first campervan in 2014 and fell in love with the campervan life, she wanted to be able to carry on cooking real food when they were out on their travels.

As she adapted and developed new campervan-friendly recipes she thought that it would be great to share these with other campers and anybody who wanted a quick easy meal for a weekday night. So Summer now blogs and writes books as The Camper Cookie, sharing her recipes and tips for the camping life.

One Last Thing...

If you enjoyed this book or found it useful I'd be very grateful if you'd post a short review on Amazon. Your support really does make a difference and I read all reviews personally so I can get your feedback and make this book even better.

Thanks again for your support!

Printed in Great Britain
by Amazon